RIDDLE-POEMS
for ages 3 to 7

GUESS THE LAST WORD

VOLUME 1

VICTOR
LANGER

Inspired by the 2019/2020
kindergarten class
called The Sunflowers
at the Berkeley Rose Waldorf
School
Berkeley, CA, USA

Table of Contents

?

A caterpillar is how I start.
You may not think I'm very smart.

But then I make a little room,
and go inside, and very soon

I come out as a different thing,
and magically I now take wing.

To visit every garden flower
And drink their nectar hour by hour.

So when you see me flutter by
you'll say, "there goes a _____".

?

I have this thing stuck on my face.
To some it may seem out of place.

Is it an arm or a leg or a nose?
It seems to have fingers, it seems to have toes.

It can pick up the tiniest thing you can see,
but it can also uproot a whole tree.

It can do almost anything you can think.
It can even suck up some water to drink.

I'm lucky to have a tool so intelligent.
Have you guessed it by now, that I am an
_____?

?

Australia's the land where I appeared,
where all the animals are really weird.

To get around quickly I like to hop.
It's faster than running, but it's harder to stop.

I carry my baby inside my pouch,
and when he kicks it makes me say ouch.

I stand on two legs and I use my tail too,
and people call me a _____.

?

I have six eyes and I'm also hairy.
To many people I'm very scary.

But I won't bite you or bother you
as long as you don't bother me too.

Just because you think I'm weird
is no reason that I should be feared.

I have eight legs and I hang from a string.
That's kind of a great and amazing thing.

I'm usually found in the yard outside,
but I may hang out in your room inside.

But whether an outsider or insider
don't hurt me just because I am a _____.

?

I'm soft and white and way up high,
just like a pillow in the sky.

I don't do much, I drift around
so quietly without a sound.

But then my shape will rearrange
and then my color too will change.

Instead of white I'll turn to gray.
This happens on a rainy day.

And then I may make lightning
which can be very frightening.

And sometimes I make thunder so loud.
You may have guessed that I'm a _____.

?

I love you all as much as can be.
That's why I'm pulling you all to me.

I'm giving you all a little tug.
It's my way of giving you all a hug.

I want you to know — you're greatly missed.
So when I pull you please don't resist.

I'm pulling you down to keep you in place,
so you don't go floating off into space.

I've been with you since the very beginning,
right under your feet, just pulling and
        spinning.

I give you the things you need to live.
Air, land and water are what I give.

I've helped you to be what you need to be,
but now it's time for you to help me.

There's nothing that has a greater worth.
Yes, I am your planet, the beautiful _____.

?

I hang out upside down all day,
but when night comes I'm on my way

to fly around (I'm not a bird)
and use my echo which can't be heard

to capture pesky flying things —
I scoop them up inside my wings.

I help you by catching lots of bugs;
so how about giving me some hugs?

You may think I have a funny face.
But I think the same of the human race.

At Halloween you picture me
with other scary things you see.

Skeletons, witches, ghosts, a black cat —
But I'm actually nice. I am a _____.

?

I can be short or I can be tall.
I can have a big tail or one that's small.

I may have a floppy or pointy ear,
and it can hear sounds that you can't hear.

And then there is my sense of smell —
It's truly amazing as you know well.

When something makes me catch a whiff
I'll follow and follow and sniff and sniff.

The mailman is sure to make me growl,
and a fire engine may make me howl.

COME, SIT and STAY are part of my training.
I usually obey without complaining.

I can help the blind and I can herd sheep.
I can guard a house without falling asleep.

I will bark and yap and whine and yelp
if someone's in trouble and needs some help.

There are so many jobs that I can do.
I can find missing things, or I can find you.

Work is okay, but I love to play.
I can run, jump and catch a Frisbee all day.

After I play I will sleep like a log.
You probably know I am called a _____.

?

I live in Africa and I'm very tall.
I like it up high. I'm not scared I might fall.

One of my favorite foods is a peach,
from the highest tree branches where others
    can't reach.

And from way up here I can easily see
any lion that's trying to sneak up on me.

People might think I look strange and might
    laugh.
But I don't care. I am called a _____.

?

I'm working, working, working all day.
I'm very important, with no time to play.

I swim with my tail — it's a big flat paddle.
In water I'm graceful, but on land I waddle.

My teeth are sharp for cutting up sticks.
I build my house with them, not with bricks.

My big front teeth can cut down a whole tree,
something you may not believe 'til you see.

When you see me at work you will be a
        believer
'cause I'm what is known as a busy _____.

?

I sneak around nightly and wear a mask.
My fingers are skillful at any task,

like opening up a garbage bin —
I'm sure to find a way to get in.

I come from the woods but I came to the town
for all of the yummy trash that's around.

You'll probably see my long striped tail
sticking out of a garbage pail.

I sleep with the sun, and I wake with the moon.
Can you guess my name? I am called a _____.

?

I have two hands but I don't have toes.
I have a face but I don't have a nose.

I'm on your desk or up high on a tower.
I always look different from hour to hour.

I tell you something without a word,
something that no one has ever heard.

The thing that I tell you is called the time.
And I'm able to ring or buzz or chime.

I can also be quiet or go tick-tock.
The thing that I am is called a _____.

?

I'm not a chicken, as you can see.
There are no feathers or wings on me.

I have floppy ears and hopping legs.
Then what am I doing with all these eggs?

And why am I hiding them all around?
The answer for this has never been found.

There's one inside the flower bed,
and one inside the garden shed.

There's one beneath the garden hose.
There might be one right under your nose.

This whole situation is rather funny.
Maybe you guessed — I'm the Easter _____.

?

We show you the way, we make it clear,
so you won't go astray, we help you steer.

We need the light for what we do;
but when it's too dark our work is through.

Like two little cameras in your face
we take a picture of a place.

We put the picture inside your mind
of things outside you that we find.

But is the picture that you see
outside or in? — Maybe both can be.

We can be brown or green or blue;
It doesn't matter for what we do.

By now it should be no surprise —
We are the ones they call your _____.

?

We like to have a lot of friends.
Our friendliness just never ends.

People may tease us for following the crowd.
But that's actually something of which we're
    proud.

The only one we're worried about
is the dog that guards us when we're out.

His barking scares us when he reminds us.
But if we should ever get lost he finds us.

We're sometimes black and sometimes white.
We don't think a color is wrong or right.

Our coat of thick and wooly hair
makes warm winter coats for you to wear.

Now we're going into the barn to sleep.
Sweet dreams from us, the sleepy _____.

?

I hide by day and I shine by night.
Sometimes I'm dim and sometimes bright.

You always ask what I can be
whenever you gaze up at me.

I live in a sky that never ends.
I have at least a billion friends.

Didn't you know that I am one
who happens to be just like your sun?

And do you wonder if there may be
some other worlds that are going round me?

But how can I be so very far? —
Well, that's my secret, for I am a _____.

?

I dive deep in the ocean with lots of power.
I can hold my breath for over an hour.

When I come to the surface I blow a big spout.
Then the people watching from the boat all
        shout.

To tell you the truth, my greatest wish
is to just eat tons and tons of fish.

My appetite has made of me
the biggest creature that swims in the sea.

They say that I should go on a diet.
I really don't want to, but maybe I'll try it.

Stand back whenever I splash my big tail.
You'll get very wet because I am a _____.

?

I have two wheels, or sometimes three.
You can have lots of fun with me.

I have two handles to hold, and a seat,
and places where you put your feet.

If you move your feet around and round
my wheels will go along the ground.

I sometimes have a horn or bell,
but if I don't you can always yell

to warn the people going past
to watch out when I'm going fast.

So please get out and take a hike,
or take a ride on me, your _____.

?

My hands are green, my feet are brown.
I stay in one place and don't travel around.

My arms are waving in the air.
I have a bird's nest in my hair.

I have a trunk and leaves and roots,
and sometimes even flowers and fruits.

I give you shade from the heat of the sun,
and climbing me is always fun.

I'm very beautiful to see.
Have you guessed it yet? I'm called a _____.

?

I'm smart and I'm friendly, I swim in the sea.
People like to hang out with me.

I can swim with a boat.
I can play with a float.

I can jump through a hoop.
I can swim in a loop.

I can dive for a ring.
I can click, I can sing.

Yes, I'll dive and I'll jump and I'll sing and I'll
     swim.
Have you guessed it by now, that I am a
    _____?

?

I'm a little motor inside your chest.
I'm always working. I never rest.

If you listen closely you'll hear a thumping.
That's actually the sound of my pumping.

I'm always pushing your blood around.
First I make it go up, then I make it go down.

It has to keep going around and through
to keep creating that thing called you.

But just as important as all the above
is that I can show you how to love.

You've probably guessed it since you're so
smart.
I'm that thing inside you that's called your
_____.

?

I fly with wings you cannot see.
Amazing! But how can it be?

The reason is that I can fly
with special wings that trick your eye.

If something happens very fast
you cannot see when it goes past.

The way you know that I'm around
is just a little humming sound.

So when the sound of humming is heard
that's sure to be a _____.

?

From a bush that's short or a tree that's tall
I spring out in spring and fall in fall.

I start out green, then I'm red, then gold
depending on whether I'm young or old.

I make my own food from the air and the sun,
then I feed other creatures with what I've
      done.

Sometimes I'm narrow and sometimes wide
like your hand when you spread it from side to
      side.

I can have either smooth or wavy edges.
I can grow on the ground or on vines or
      hedges.

How many of me is beyond belief.
Wherever you look you will see a _____.

?

I'm very rude and I have bad manners.
All that I care about is bananas.

If I have a banana and so do you
I'll try to steal yours so that I can have two.

If you ever come to visit the zoo
watch out for your lunch — I may steal that
     too.

I'm nervous and always jumping around
in the treetops and on the ground.

People are sometimes ashamed to say
they're related to me in any way.

You're wrong if you guessed that I am a
     donkey.
Because what I really am is a _____.

?

Sometimes I'm round and sometimes thin.
I always end where I begin.

And sometimes I will go away,
but I'll come back on another day.

You always know exactly when,
for after a month I start again.

You may think that I'm very bright
the way that I light up the night;

but actually that light you see
is just the sun's light bouncing off me.

Spinning around your world is my business.
(It doesn't cause me any dizziness.)

You may think that I look like an orange
     balloon,
but I am the one that is called the _____.

?

I can see when there's hardly any light,
even on a cloudy and moonless night.

I can fly through tree branches and close to the
        ground
without even making the tiniest sound.

I can turn my head almost all the way 'round
to find whatever there is to be found.

People think I am very wise
because of my big and serious eyes.

I have an angry look that is called a scowl.
But I'm really not mean. I am just an _____.

?

I'm the shape of a window, and the shape of a
    wall,
I'm the shape of the pictures that hang in the
    hall.

I'm the shape of a slice of cheese or bread,
and the shape of the blanket that's on your
    bed.

I'm the shape of the ceiling, the shape of the
    floor,
the shape of a rug, and a garage door.

I'm the shape of a table and the shape of a
    book.
I'm the shape of most things wherever you
    look.

Why is it that almost everywhere
so many things have the shape of a _____?

?

I scamper around among the tree branches.
I make daring jumps and I take lots of chances.

You may think I'm living dangerously,
but have you ever seen me fall from a tree?

My long fluffy tail is always wagging.
I'm the world's greatest acrobat — maybe I'm
        bragging.

I can climb head-first down the trunk of a tree.
My claws let me do that, amazingly.

I can also run faster than fast can be.
Your dog will never catch up with me.

I can walk on top of the narrowest fences.
I can get around your bird feeder's defenses.

But I wish I had thumbs like you people do.
Then I'd hold a nut with one hand, not two.

I'm usually gray but sometimes I'm red.
A boy doesn't have any horns on his head —

So you can't tell if I am a boy or a girl.
But one thing you know is that I am a _____.

?

When you go to sleep at night
I'm always with you and I might

be holding you in every dream
when nothing is what it may seem.

When you're home from school because you're
    sick
I help you to fell better quick.

When you're tired and you need a rest
I'm right there beneath you — a cozy nest.

But I'm not just for resting as you have seen;
I'm also good as a trampoline.

When night comes again and you rest your
    head,
you rest it on me. I am your _____.

?

I make it light so you can see,
but please don't look directly at me.

I light up objects with my light,
but by myself I'm much too bright.

Because of me a shadow is made
unless you're standing in the shade.

I'm always sending out rays all day
except when a cloud is in the way.

If you lie on the beach make sure you turn.
Otherwise I may give you a burn.

I feel nice and warm, but I'm sometimes too
      hot,
so if it's uncomfortable change your spot.

You used to think I set and rise
but then you learned to your surprise

that things are not what they seem to be —
It's *you* who are really going round *me*.

My light gives life to everyone.
Can you guess my name? I am the _____.

?

Don't pet me because you might think I'm a
    cat.
You don't want to make a mistake like that.

I don't use my claws to protect myself well.
Instead I use my horrible smell.

Don't try to be nice, for whatever you think,
if you make me afraid I will cause a big stink.

Just leave me alone in the trash and the junk.
Please keep far away, because I am a _____.

?

I wear tree branches on my head.
I'm famous for pulling Santa's sled.

My seven friends and I
pull Santa's sled across the sky.

If it doesn't snow, then we don't care
because his sled goes in the air.

Children are listening on the ground
for our sleigh bells' jingling sound.

Then when we suddenly appear
they all shout, "There go Santa's _____."

?

I'm sitting here inside your head
I'm gray and wrinkled, but don't be misled:

It's true, I may not look like much,
but I can see-hear-smell-taste-touch.

I do all five, amazingly,
and I do it all electrically.

Whenever messages come to me
I figure out what they can be.

I then decide what's false and true
and then I tell you what to do.

I watch for the body's pleasure and pain.
I'm on the job. I am your _____.

?

I'm the most boring animal that there can be.
Who would want to write a poem about me?

If you're looking for a creature that's fun
then probably I am not the one.

I just stand around for most of the day.
Or I may lie down for a while in the hay.

There's very little that I actually do.
But once in a while I may say "moo."

You probably have guessed it by now.
I'm the one that people call a _____.

?

I bring you news from far away
and tell you the weather for today.

I'm a game and a movie, and what is more,
I even can be your favorite store.

I sing you a song, I show you a map,
and all you do is click or tap.

I give you words and pictures too.
There is so much that I can do.

So can you think of anything cuter
than your user-friendly home _____?

?

My smell and colors are sure to please,
but I can also make you sneeze

in case you have some allergies,
and also you have to watch out for bees.

So before you stick your nose in me
make sure that I'm not hiding a bee

that may be inside where you cannot see
so smell me very carefully.

Enjoy my beauty at any hour.
I'm proud to be what is called a _____.

?

I'm used whenever people are meeting,
and also whenever people are greeting.

I can wave goodbye or wave hello.
I can point to something above or below.

Sometimes music will make me snap.
If I really like it then I may even clap.

I can thread a needle — that's hard to do.
I wonder if a robot can too.

I can pull out a splinter or pull out a drawer;
I can open a window or open a door.

No other tool is so useful and
as totally handy as your _____.

?

I'm always cleaning my whiskers and fur.
If you pet me nicely it makes me purr.

My claws are sharp and I can scratch.
I hunt to see what I can catch.

Or I sit around all day in the sun.
Doing nothing is also fun.

I like it whenever you rub my tummy
or give me some tuna fish so yummy.

But don't give me too much or I'll get fat.
That's the way I am because I am a _____.

?

Some women are afraid of me,
but children think I'm cute as can be.

Whenever I give a little squeak
it's sure to make somebody say, "Eek!"

Some people want me to go away.
But other people want me to stay.

I have a whiskery twitchy nose.
It twitches and sniffs wherever it goes.

I'm usually found outside on the ground,
hiding or digging or running around.

But sometimes I'll sneak inside your house.
Then someone may say, "We've got a _____."

?

I am the garden where you grew.
You were once hidden inside me, too.

Then you appeared, a little sprout.
Instead of in you now were out.

I watered you, and every day
I carefully kept the weeds away.

You turned into a little tree
and spread your arms so happily.

You grew so big you even made
the garden stand inside your shade.

A separate thing you seem to be,
but really you're still part of me.

So who am I? I am none other
than the one that's called your _____.

About the Author

Victor Langer is a freelance writer
and graphic designer
in the San Francisco area.
His other books are:

More Riddle Poems for ages 3 to 7
(volume 2)
1040 for Dogs, and other tax forms
Logo Coloring Book
Crop Circle Coloring Book
Insect Coloring Book
Multiple-Universe Multiple-Choice
Geriacula, the Senile Vampire

His books have received praise in *The New York Times, The Wall Street Journal, The New York Daily News,* and *New York Magazine.*

Printed in Great Britain
by Amazon